night
haunting

Robert Grant

CREATIVE FUTURE
empowering marginalised artists and writers

First published 2015
Creative Future
Community Base
113 Queens Road
Brighton BN1 3XG
01273 234780
info@creativefuture.org.uk
www.creativefuture.org.uk
facebook.com/creativefuture
twitter @CreativeF_uture

ISBN 978-0-9932333-0-2

LOTTERY FUNDED

Supported using public funding by

ARTS COUNCIL ENGLAND

Money raised by
HealthWish
through

For my mother

I would like to thank Dominique, Niamh and Vicki, as well as all at Creative Future, for their hard work and endeavour, and, especially, Dr. Claudia Gould for her tireless belief, inspiration and guidance. All without which this work would not have been made possible.

Contents

Foreword

Robert Grant comes into print a new voice, but one that looks to old forms of poetic expression. There is a familiar resonance to the sound of his verse, although the subjects – homelessness, poverty, madness and the soulless, impenetrable skin of bureaucracy – feel searingly contemporary. The old topics – loneliness, death and love – are here, too. Shelley would recognise them all.

Robert observes Ezra Pound's dictum that "No vers is libre for the man who wants to do a good job" and keeps to sonnet, triolet, villanelle and other countable forms, finding freedom within the constraints of measured verse, pleased (with Wordsworth) "if some Souls . . . who have felt the weight of too much liberty should find brief solace there".

Solace perhaps, but perturbation as well; regular scansion does not ensure regularity of life or viewpoint. Robert's dark dreams will trouble the reader, as does any fully realised poetry. The constant argument between the seemliness – even playfulness – of the shape and language of the poems and their subversive content is one of the chief pleasures of reading Robert Grant's work. The play between repetition and surprise occurs in every piece, demanding of the reader a flexibility of response to match the poet's own.

His is work old-fashioned in its craftsman-like construction, modern in its unflinching eye.

From the reproachful anger at friendship betrayed of 'Fool', to the fantastic curiosity of 'Lake Tahoe' and the sharp seaside observation of 'Gull', Robert Grant takes his readers through their worlds and his own, a confident guide, firmly stepping through sorrow, humour and phantasmagoria, relying upon the tools which have served generations of poets before him.

DR. CLAUDIA GOULD

Wooden Buddha

A wooden Buddha sits upon my shelf,
So ignorant of books and magazines,
And DVDs in racks, all neatly cleaned.
He sits and thinks of nothing but himself,
This Buddha bought for spiritual wealth.
He never sleeps, nor tries to let off steam,
But meditates a lonely Buddha's dream
Of preservation, carved with Nature's stealth.

No rocks, nor murky ponds, all spilt with mud,
Could shake this sculptured icon from his form.
No wars, nor burglars thieving for their drugs,
Or shadows of apocalyptic storms
Could ever make his body stretch and yawn,
But, motionless, he dreams himself in blood.

Man in City Garden

(Scandal)

The pathways always seem so busy now
The winter sun has dipped, so cold and dark,
The skies so grey and vague, so *anyhow*,
And shadows dankly spreading on the park.
He walks, head down, his mind on other days,
A wrinkled frown, eyes blinded by the haze.
A man who lived his life so bright and stark;
A man reliant upon others' praise.

At times, he stops to think about the past:
How everything seemed clearer in his youth –
A future known, as everything was classed
And exercised according to his truth;
How everything was simple, neat and clean
Before the years had stripped him, bare and lean.

      Before his world was seen

As something so infernal, so unwashed,
And wrung out, like a shabby, wretched cloth.

Constant Occupation

Constant occupation tends to kill
What spirit the survivor has inside.
Used, by force, against his creed and will,
Shuffling with a fallen, broken stride.

What spirit the survivor has inside,
Aching with his seeping fortitude,
Shuffling with a fallen, broken stride,
Sits within his lies of gratitude.

Aching with his seeping fortitude,
The worker keeps his eyes towards the ground,
Sits within his lies of gratitude
And never dares to make a muttered sound.

The worker keeps his eyes towards the ground,
Thinking of his family and his past
And never dares to make a muttered sound
In case some lost complaint should be his last.

Thinking of his family and his past,
He ruminates at what has come to be
In case some lost complaint should be his last:
A sacrifice in longing to be free.

He ruminates at what has come to be,
Used, by force, against his creed and will;
A sacrifice in longing to be free –
Constant occupation tends to kill.

The Blizzard

Could any of us question what we'd seen
That night the blizzard swept us from the road?
Redigging tracks and knocking shovels clean,
Could any of us question what we'd seen?
The frozen winds blew ice on where we'd been;
We huddled close, in silence, as we rode.
Could any of us question what we'd seen
That night the blizzard swept us from the road?

Silly Games

A part of him enjoyed their silly games,
The blending of a man into a god,
And breaking down what spirit still remained.

Instead of being cured, his soul was lame
And, though he found it difficult and odd,
A part of him enjoyed their silly games.

Across the vanquished streets, where walls were stained
With blood from beatings of the whip and rod
And breaking down what spirit still remained,

Where courtiers and censors fed the flames
Down alleyways, where prisoners had stood,
A part of him enjoyed their silly games.

Creating some small myth for hope and change,
The politicians wept for wash and flood
And breaking down what spirit still remained.

And even as he slept, they stole his name
As every trace of light went out for good.
A part of him enjoyed their silly games
And breaking down what spirit still remained.

Night Haunting

I do not want to live here any more,
At night I hear strange noises from upstairs.
The attic creeps, there's scratching on the floor
And something seems to push the rocking chair.

At night I hear strange noises from upstairs:
A whisper here, some laughter in the night.
And something seems to push the rocking chair
And giggles when I reach the landing height.

A whisper here. Some laughter in the night.
A weight upon the bed, a hand that feels,
And giggles, when I reach the landing height.
Though part of me still says, '*It isn't real.*'

A weight upon the bed. A hand that feels.
A movement, as I hide myself away.
Though part of me still says, '*It isn't real,*'
I stand alone in corners and I pray.

A movement, as I hide myself away.
An eye that catches shadows as I stare.
I stand alone in corners and I pray,
And no one else will know I'm ever there.

An eye that catches shadows as I stare
Until the passing hours are dull and grey.
And no one else will know I'm ever there
Until the dark bled night becomes the day.

Until the passing hours are dull and grey
The attic creeps. There's scratching on the floor.
Until the dark bled night becomes the day
I do not want to live here any more.

Jocasta

When scars that travel fast should run so deep,
Am I the one to shake these scales of fear?
What motion, what enslaves this mother's sleep
When, marching on, each storm cloud brings him near?

Between these pearls I hear the scattered news,
The battles and the strength within his core.
Between my words I pray for life anew
Within my breast, beyond the seeds of war.

What kind of king would enter at my gate?
A bloodless man, a prince, unjust, unsure?
What kind of man could furnish so much hate,
Yet take a wife and throne, as one before?

A riddle, like a demon in his hands,
Now set to purify these wasted lands.

What surrogate, what Man

Within these scented chambers waits his throne?
Now kindled to our fortunes, to mine own.

Self Help

He talks about a search for something else:
A lecture on the spirit and its themes.
He talks and talks of nothing but himself.

Some comments on a culture, thieved from shelves,
But, in his mind, he owns its mode and means.
He talks about a search for something else.

Compromising practises for wealth,
To bask in being heard and being seen,
He talks and talks of nothing but himself.

As students listen for success and health,
Or praying that some other truth is gleaned,
He talks about a search for something else.

And, listening very little to their help –
The eyes that shine, the bodies starved and lean –
He talks and talks of nothing but himself.

Despite his wit, despite some presence felt
By those who'd beg for hope, he struts and preens.
He talks about a search for something else.
He talks and talks of nothing but himself.

Narcissus' Body

Narcissus shook the body by the throat,
Some backwards screaming slip of gypsy wretch,
Who would not disappear and could not float,
But gathered all the tears his eyes had wept.
A struggle, life dissected by its means,
Reflecting what self-hatred had begun.
A dream of life was lost inside a dream:
Another world had lost another son.

Our weary world looked on.

Rust. Apartheid. Lurid breath grew fuller
Than when the secret service praised police.
The politicians hid their lies and laughter
Behind the stony silence of the priests.
And, borrowing a guess to what was true,
Some second nature's coming, some lost colour,
In death the blackest boy was coloured blue.

About the Others

No one wants to know about the others,
Those voices who are screaming in my head –
They'd rather think about their blood and brothers:
No one wants to hear about the others.

They'd like to fantasise about their lovers,
The ones to whom they'd pledged the love, they said,
Would welcome them as fathers or as mothers –
No one wants to hear about the others.

The visitors, the children, under covers,
Who, cowering, uptight, are filled with dread,
They wish for loving sisters and for brothers.
No one wants to hear about the others.

And everyone would rather push or shove us
Between their lies and language of the dead,
The ones who'd crawl below or glide above us –
No one wants to hear about the others,
Those voices who are screaming in my head.

Sane

I lost the plot completely when they came:
Two officers, two doctors and a nurse.
They might as well have brought the funeral hearse,
Or have me shot like some old horse that's lame.
They asked me lots of questions, then my name,
Then all about my scribbles and my verse,
And did I really think that I was cursed?
The panic in me helped me to explain

That everything I wrote was meant to be
An outlet for my own creative urge,
To help me find the peace I need to gain
Within a world with shackled liberties.
So, if I write a sonnet or a dirge,
Who are they to say that I'm insane?

She Was the Best Thing

She was the best thing,
Her sweets, her sweat.
She was the first thing.

Skin all firm and tight,
She was the light,
She was the best thing.

And hair, tumbling in locks,
Fallen brown, brunette,
Unaware of her testing.

She was the best thing.
Scents so sweet
From toes to fingers,
From eyelashes to feet,

I kissed and miss them all now.
She was the best thing

So sweet.

The Closing Wound

Studying your deep and sparkling eyes,
Flinching, where the flames enlist your pupils,
I listen as my mouth begins to lie
Once more and think, *how could I be so stupid?*

Breaking, though your sobbing turns so soon
To rhapsodies I cannot hear nor touch,
I step aside beyond your closing wounds,
To realise how words can hurt so much.

Remembering the things we'd never had
Nor should have had, if worlds are so apart
That bridging them in fantasies seemed mad,
As faith and madness breed a finer art.

If life is art, then let your art belong
To every faith and heart that keeps you strong.

      I know I did you wrong.

As, studying your deepest, sparkling eyes,
I understand how loss has made me lie.

Friday

Friday is the night when they make love
Across the street, their curtains opened wide.
Between the terraces, fit warm and snug,
Friday is the night when they make love.
Both entwined, like fingers of a glove,
Two lovers, both responding, side by side.
Friday is the night when they make love
Across the street, their curtains opened wide.

Two and a Half Years

Two and a half years of being alone;
No contact returned, not even a letter.
Nobody speaks or picks up a phone,
Two and a half years of being alone.
The heart dries as hard as water on stone
And, every day, *more!* And, *things will get better!*
Two and a half years of being alone.
No contact returned, not even a letter.

Darker Places

I guess that you are thinking you know me,
Or that you understand this thing I do.
Maybe, within some ways, your thoughts are true
And maybe you can grasp my poetry.
Perhaps you think that verse should surely be
About describing lovers, or those who
Had their dreams ungainly blown askew,
Or things like blossomed hills or rolling seas…

But each of us has something deep inside
That draws the heart into a different place;
A memory, an act could be a clue
To circumstances where you'd duly lied.
Perhaps, in here, you'll find a different trace,
And I have darker places yet for you…

Waterbelly Lane

Keep on down that backward road,
She said, between the stars.
And so we drove throughout the night
Away from prison bars.

Keep on down those downward streets
That always look the same.
And so we went where we would meet
Down Waterbelly Lane.

We moved until the morning light
Where once our love had thrived.
We moved until the morning light
To keep our hearts alive.

She'd said we'd have such little time
Before they all would come
And seek us out beyond the lines
Of wayward, rising suns.

She said the fallow horses run
To catch the crescent moon.
A bloody star, a harvest sun:
More blood was coming soon.

We stood until the morning light.
We stood where we had thrived.
We stood until the morning light
To keep our hearts alive.

We stood a while and raced on through
Down highways we had feared.
And, never stopping when they called,
Towards that band we steered.

And so, it came, before the flanks,
Their cars all looked the same.
We broke their ranks and broke the bank
Down Waterbelly Lane.

Now, stand until the morning light
And stand where we had thrived;
Stand until the morning light
To keep your hearts alive.

And raise your hands before your eyes
And catch the distant sun,
And see your world uncompromised
And feel your life begun.

See your life uncompromised
Where streets all look the same.
And drive on through those wayward ranks
Down Waterbelly Lane.

Scissor, Paper, Stone

This is how I journey through the space
That time allows our bodies to perceive,
In falls of autumn branches, falls of leaves,
Inside this universe's growing face.
This is how I journey through our race:
A place of pleasantries, a place of Man,
A place where all the best do what they can.
A place where our uncertainty is traced.

I travel, reeling north, between the stars –
Stone gilded on the rocks of burning suns –
A split of light, a shiver past the moon:
A walker wakened past his prison bars.
Scissor, stone and paper help me run
And document my journey with a swoon.

    Time always comes too soon

To say that we were here, conjoined, alone.
And nothing blunts these scissors more than stone.

Fool

He spoke his mind with little sympathy.
He could not care about my state of mind,
Or that the words he spoke were of the kind
That made me feel my life's futility.
He couldn't give a toss for empathy,
Nor mental health, nor being so unkind
By saying things so harsh they'd leave you blind.
His nature couldn't take uncertainty.

★

I'm full of praise for everyone I know.
Manners mean so much to me, you see.
And rudeness is unquestionably cruel.
I've changed my mind, so now I'll have to grow
A thicker skin for dull formalities.
Because, I think I've been some kind of fool.

The Father Thing

(a villanelle for Philip K. Dick)

So, was it just the father thing you owned,
Or did you make your peace in other ways,
Where fiction and psychosis claimed your throne?

A scatterer, a scanner, light and loaned
For all unsightly settlers in this maze;
So, was it just the father thing you owned?

Or were those regal memories you'd sown
Conspiracies for lonely travelled days
Where fiction and psychosis claimed your throne?

A genius, in some forgotten home,
For intellects and paranoids and strays.
So, was it just the father thing you owned?

Nobody who could question what you'd known
Would ever dare to take the flight you'd made,
Where fiction and psychosis claimed your throne.

And we could never stand as clowns or clones
Or entertainers, searching for some praise.
So, was it just the father thing you owned,
Where fiction and psychosis claimed your throne?

The Library Police

(a villanelle for Stephen King)

We wait before the library police.
A line of us down some long corridor,
In ignorance and pride and in belief.

A jacket torn, a coffee stain or crease,
A page unduly ripped, a cover worn.
We wait before the library police,

Held silent under signs requesting 'Peace',
But in a room another oath is sworn
In ignorance and pride and in belief.

An echo here, a plea, a scream released,
A table tilted down, some water drawn.
We wait before the library police,

Stood side by side, the boy, the clerk, the thief,
But one of us will die before the dawn
In ignorance and pride and in belief.

No silence is so certain in its grief
For petty crimes and torturers and law.
We wait before the library police
In ignorance and pride and in belief.

The Freak

If he could have met with an accident,
Paralysed his face or shredded a limb,
Or slipped into hot oil and peeled his skin,
He might have understood what pride had meant.

Instead, his sickest parts cannot be seen.
At night he slumps, next to a kitchen bin,
And slurs, inebriated, through a grin:
'This freak, for everyone, is better dead.'

It's not as if his mind lacks the intent
To throw misfortune in a quick lime cage,
Enraged and rattled, rotting through the earth.
It's only that his twisted mind is spent,
Exhausted at the strength required to change,
Where changing steals his greatest efforts first.

      To rectify his brain.

Rearranging the pride that cannot speak
And let redemption burn within the freak.

Gull

Foot bent back, yellow and long,
Three toes webbed, crooked and thin;
There is no tune to your blistering song,
There is no joy in the news that you bring.
Fledgling, from chick to bird, you fight:
Wise in old age, uncaring in youth.
A wing on the sky, a scrounger in flight,
A pecker for everything, that is your truth.

But some may see your beauty, even yet:
The flick of your feathers, the curve of your gut,
The strength of the muscles that twist in your neck,
The arcing to rise by the tip of your foot;
Breaking the edge of the winds to fly,
This is your nature, until you die.

I Saw a Clay Red Horse

I saw a clay red horse leap from a tower
Of chalk white lining, upright, like a bolt
Of lightning in the night. Such grace; such power.
I saw a clay red horse leap from a tower.
The cobalt sky bled warmth, the stars a shower
Of iridescent light behind the colt.
I saw a clay red horse leap from a tower
Of chalk white lining, upright, like a bolt.

On Rhyming

Your rhymes are far too easy for my taste,
And, don't you know, they've all been done before.
For someone such as you, it's such a waste.

I must have seen a thousand like your case,
And reading them is such a thankless chore.
Your rhymes are far too easy for my taste.

Nobody gives a jot for rhyme, nor pace,
And rhyming's for the nursery – no more!
For someone such as you, it's such a waste.

To think your self-belief was so misplaced,
Perhaps there's something else you could explore?
Your rhymes are far too easy for my taste.

Forgive me if I seem somewhat barefaced,
But, really, all this *rhyming's* such a bore!
For someone such as you, it's such a waste.

In modern verse it's just a damned disgrace
And poetry is after… *something more.*
Your rhymes are far too easy for my taste,
For someone such as you, it's such a waste.

Lake Tahoe

Oh, what did you see, Mr. Cousteau,
Down at the bottom of Lake Tahoe?
Did you see demons, did you see death,
Did screaming escape from the sound of your breath?

Were you so ashen that words could not come?
Did your heart beat like the sound of a drum?
Were you left gasping, studied in shock?
Did something flash out from under Cave Rock?

Did something stir from the mud and the silt?
Were you left reeling in panic and guilt
For something forbidden and so far unseen?
And did you suppress the sound of a scream?

Did the Calypso come to your mind,
With weights and bottles? Were you left blind
Through terror and tremors and shaking and fear?
Did you lose faith in all you held dear?

Could you imagine a greater surprise –
Did something stare back with roll-around eyes
And leathery back and mouth of chalk white?
Were you left frozen, bound up with fright?

Did you pull up, gasping for air,
Running your fingers through grey, thinning hair?
Did you sit thinking, *What have I done?*
Under the waters, far from the sun?

Did breathing and scuba hold still in your head,
As sonar pings echoed some sounds full of dread?
Did you think back to your family and wife?
Were you in fear for the days of your life?

Did something move quickly, there, down below?
Oh, what did you see, Mr. Cousteau?

Did massive shapes wash by the blink of an eye?
Did you hide data, protecting a lie?
Did you see creatures, thought of long gone?
Did something there prove that we all were wrong?

Did you pray quickly, silent, sincere?
Did something ring out and sharpen your ear?
Did you resurface and say with regret,
'The world is not ready for what's down there, yet.'

Oh, what did you see, Mr. Cousteau,
Down at the bottom of Lake Tahoe?
Did you see demons? Did you see death?
And did they all haunt your nightmares, your breath?

Pyre

Walking through the dust cloud of your dreams,
I step along and reconcile my thoughts:
How everything you'd planned had come to nought,
Embittered and so battled at your schemes.
Your robbery, your tactics and your themes –
All along I knew the things you'd sought,
But gave them no regard till you were caught.
I moved on down as thunder stirred and teemed.

★

Nothing, now, shall matter any more.
Our lives are wildernesses, burnt and cleared.
And prophecies from you taste of the fire
That piles the charcoal bricks up by the score.
Your promises were nothing without fear.
And everything but wealth burns on the pyre.

I Thought of You

I thought of you, upon the train,
Travelling through those sheets of rain,
Travelling there to journey home
So wistful and so all alone.
So resigned and so in vain.

The drizzle wept upon each pane,
And ran down them in dirty stains,
Dripped upon the steel and chrome;
                  I thought of you.

Your vision, then, had so remained
Inside my mind, and so ingrained;
Heavy, like a weight of stone
Tossed before a grey sea foam.
I journeyed on, but then, again,
                  I thought of you.

Oh, Orpheus!

Oh, Orpheus, my boy, what have you done?
The seasons are retreating from their lease
And everywhere is dark, no light, no sun,
Just memories of summer's haze and peace.

The seasons are retreating from their lease,
Enforcers, like the doubts you had in mind,
Just memories of summer's haze and peace,
Regretting every chance and every lie.

Enforcers, like the doubts you had in mind,
The songs you made, the melancholy sound,
Regretting every chance and every lie,
Regretting that last time you turned around.

The songs you made, the melancholy sounds,
Now sweep your victories to loss and grave,
Regretting that last time you turned around,
Regretting every journey that you made.

Now, sweep your victories to loss and grave.
And everywhere is dark, no light, no sun,
Regretting every journey that you made:
Oh, Orpheus, my boy, what have you done?

Never Have Them Say

Never have them say it was in vain,
Those people who would put you to one side.
Wisdom only comes through love and pain.

The gamblers, who would sell you for some gain
And profit from your loses, only lied.
Never have them say it was in vain.

The drivers, who would ride that stubborn train
And brake for nothing, surely turn and sigh,
'Wisdom only comes through love and pain.'

The standard bearers, running through the rain
Till muscles ache with weariness and pride,
Never have them say it was in vain.

In all of those who live through strife and strain
With hearts that beat with longingness inside:
Wisdom only comes through love and pain.

So now, my dearest dear, my strongest chain,
My emptiness, my chasm tearing wide,
Never have them say it was in vain:
Wisdom only comes through love and pain.

Slowly Going Nowhere

Reaching out my fingers from the past
I drag my weight upon the muddy shore,
Slowly going nowhere very fast.

Taking time to breathe in violent gasps
And focussing my mind on something more,
Reaching out my fingers from the past.

The truth is left uncertain, only paths
That cross my memories are stored,
Slowly going nowhere very fast.

The earth is dark and dense, the planet cast
Into a universe without a core.
Reaching out my fingers from the past

I hold to what I find, my sense as vast
As anything that evolution spores,
Slowly going nowhere very fast.

And, knowing that no night is first or last,
I crush my hand between my tccth and gnaw,
Reaching out my fingers from the past,
Slowly going nowhere very fast.

Snow

Even as the heavens darkly melted,
Even as the skies began to grow
Heavy with the crystals that they pelted,
Even as the sky struck up with snow,

Many of our footprints vanished brightly,
Soft and shuffled, useless guides to home.
Many of them filled their hollows nightly,
As many of us lost our ways in snow.

Pathways that for years had seen us keeping
Welcome hearths for those who come and go,
Villagers have lost, despite their sweeping
As villages were lost within the snow.

Even as we shouted out our warnings
The blizzards wept and blinded us again.

How could we ever know?

Somewhere, as I heard your echoes calling,
I stood my ground and lost myself in snow.

Flesh and Blood

Give them all your heart, your flesh and blood,
Tell them of the place where you once stood.
Show them all your life, your mind, your eyes,
Fill them with those stories of surprise.

Tell them, as a man, how once you lived
A sufferer for reason; what you did
For government, for cause, in pain and grief;
Tell them how they stole your self-belief

But took it on, in duty, for a world
That doesn't know the truth, that's never heard.
Tell them, in your age, how you acquired
A reason to stay hid and unadmired.

Remind them of the fact it wasn't fun
Standing in the sights of someone's gun.
And let them know, through every word and line
There never was a time you felt 'just fine'.

Tell them that your earth has gone to seed,
That every time you speak you slowly bleed.